www.thedailygraceco.com

CONTRIBUTORS

....

Illustrator:
KATIE GRACE WILL

Editors:
HELEN HUMMEL
ALLI TURNER
JENNIE HEIDEMAN

How to Read this Book

Mommy Lost a Baby: Emma's Hope in Grief is a book about a little girl whose mommy experiences a pregnancy loss. When the baby dies, her mommy is very sad, and together, they learn how to process their grief as a family.

If you have recently experienced a pregnancy loss, it may be difficult for you to read this book without crying. That's okay. Tears are a healthy part of the grieving process. Similarly, if you are reading this book with a child, it may be helpful to warn your child that you may cry and give them permission to express any emotions they may have.

At the same time, children process grief in different ways. If your child is very young, he or she may not understand the concept of death. That, too, is okay. You don't need to make your child understand the loss of the baby before he or she is developmentally ready. This book can be saved as a resource for future conversations when your child is older.

With older children, you may find that your child lands somewhere on the emotional spectrum of grief, ranging from feeling very sad to emotionally disconnected from the loss. Your child may be confused about why God allowed their baby brother or sister to die, and he or she may have difficult questions about death. Our prayer is that this book opens the door to fruitful conversations about the hope of the gospel, even through the tragedy of pregnancy loss.

Because of the cross, we know that God understands our pain. We can be honest with our emotions and bring all of them to the Lord. Although the sting of death may pierce deeply today, one day, God will heal every wound. He is coming again to make all things right.

Helping Your Child Process Grief

Children experience grief in different ways. Consider the following as you seek to help your child process through grief:

1   Many young children process grief through play. They may color pictures or imagine doctors' appointments as they play with their dolls. As you seek to love your child after the loss of a baby, enter into his or her world. Pick up a crayon and color together, seeking loving conversation as you draw.

2   Children process grief in different ways. Some children respond to pain by acting strong or by being on their best behavior. Meanwhile, they may be internalizing the loss of their sibling or wondering if the pregnancy loss is somehow their fault because they weren't excited to share their toys. Other children may feel confused that Mommy is crying or wonder if they did something wrong. They may rebel with tantrums and unexpected battles, or they may ask the same questions over and over in order to make sense of the loss. As much as possible, be a good student of your child. Be patient with him or her, and provide a safe space for your child to process his or her emotions by asking them good questions. Sample questions can be found at the end of this book.

3   An emotions chart can be a helpful tool to help young children process their emotions. An emotions chart is a chart with different faces that display different kinds of emotions. There is an emotions chart in the back of the book for you to use as a tool to help your child. Ask your child to point to the emotion that he or she is feeling. Name the emotion for him or her, and ask why he or she is feeling that way. If your child is not sure why he or she is feeling that way, that is okay. Sometimes, just expressing the emotion can be the beginning of understanding our feelings.

God's Word speaks to our emotions. When we are able to express how we feel, we not only grow in our emotional intelligence, but we also can find comfort in the Scriptures. We discover that the Bible speaks about sadness, confusion, fear, and more. For more information about expressing emotions through grief, see The Daily Grace Co.'s *Gospel Hope in Grief* booklet.

4   As older children process the death of a baby, they often have difficult questions about God's goodness and sovereignty. With these difficult questions, it is okay to say, "I don't know," and dive into Scripture later to learn more.

Emma is four. She loves ice cream and cake.
She loves puppies, rainbows, and friends.
She loves painting and twirling around and around,
till she wobbles and bobbles and bends.

She loves cuddles and books with her parents.
She loves cold, sticky popsicles, too.
When she turns five, her one birthday wish
is to go see the bears at the zoo!

Emma was told some great news by her dad
while at breakfast one sunshiny day.
"Your mom is expecting a new baby boy.
His birthday is a few months away!"

"Mommy is having a baby!" she cried.
"I can't wait for us to be friends.
We'll run and play games. We'll paint and do chalk.
We'll dress up and then play pretend."

We'll build magical worlds in our games fit for two,
with castles and dragons of all different hues.
He'll be the brave prince, and I will be the great queen.
So throughout the weeks, Emma's dreams grew and grew.

Young Emma created a beautiful plan,
about the adventures they'd share.
They'd draw pictures, do puzzles, and plan silly pranks.
They'd be an inseparable pair.

She loved holding her hand against Mommy's skin
and feeling his sweet little taps.
She'd sit and imagine his small little toes
and a smile on his face while he napped.

Then Mommy sat next to young Emma one night.
She had a big tear in her eye.
What happened? Emma wondered. *And why's Mom so sad?*
So sad Emma wanted to cry.

"We lost the baby," Mom said with a sigh;
she groaned with a crumpled-up face.
"I don't understand," Emma said slowly.
"A baby you can't just... misplace?"

What does that mean? And where is he now?
are thoughts Emma wanted to say.
But when she saw Mom begin to cry,
she gave her a hug right away.

Mom said that the baby had died in the night;
she went to the doctor today.
Emma took a big breath. She'd try to be strong.
She'd help out her mom right away.

Throughout the next week, her mom was still sad;
she'd cry and spend time all alone.
Emma was good, and she tried to obey,
to help and clean up on her own.

But Emma still missed her brother a lot.
Her questions continued to grow:
How did he die? Will it happen again?
Why did he die? Where did he go?

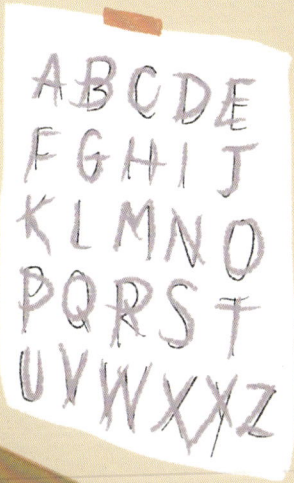

She missed feeling his kicks. She missed happy days.
She missed what would never become.
She missed all her dreams. She missed how things were.
She felt sad, confused, and undone.

Then one night at bedtime, she started to cry
when she thought of her plans once so great—
of parties and pillow fights and games at the park.
Her plans now would just have to wait.

Her mom heard her sobbing and came right away;
together they hugged, and they cried.
But she didn't want her mom to be sad,
so she pulled back and then tried to hide.

Her mom gently whispered, "I know that this hurts.
It's okay to be mad and to grieve.
You don't have to be strong. It's okay to be sad."
And she wiped Emma's tears on her sleeve.

EMMA

"This world is so broken, and sometimes it hurts.
We get boo-boos and lose those we love.
And when we feel sad, alone, or confused,
we can pray and get help from above."

"When God made the world, He made it so good,
but sin came to earth with the fall.
And with sin came death and sadness and tears,
and brokenness covered it all."

"But God saw His children in all of our hurt.
He loved us, and He made a plan.
He'd send us a Savior who'd come to the world—
His own Son, who's both God and man!"

"And so Jesus came and entered our world;
He was faithful, loving, and true.
He was just like us, with boo-boos and scrapes,
but He was perfectly good too."

"He knows what it means to go through big pain;
He came as a payment for sin.
He hung on the cross; He suffered and died,
but He came alive once again!"

"This Jesus is with us. He cries with us too.
He will never leave us alone.
He loves us and prays for us in all of our pain;
He holds us, and our grief is known."

"And not only this, He is coming again!
He'll make all things right one day, too.
He has a great plan, and He'll make all things new;
we trust that He'll always come through."

"I don't have the answers," her mom then said slowly,
"but I do know that God is still good.
We can talk to Him, cry out, and tell Him our pain.
We can share it with Him, and we should."

Her dad then walked in and gave Emma a hug.
He said, "You are never alone.
It's okay to cry and ask questions galore.
Remember: you're loved, and you're known."

"Not only this," her dad then continued,
"but I miss your baby brother too.
I want to protect you—to be brave and strong.
But even brave men feel sad like you."

So together, they made another great plan
for how to remember the baby.
They'd mention his name and get him a stocking
with a handsome prince dressed in navy.

Their family continued to talk as they grieved,
sharing their thoughts and their fears too.
They remembered that Jesus is coming again
and prayed when they were feeling blue.

So if you're a sibling who also is sad,
you don't have to be on your own.
Cry out to God; tell your parents how you feel.
Remember: you're never alone.

When King Jesus comes, He'll make all things right!
He'll wipe every tear from our eyes.
There'll be no more pain or suffering or death;
we'll see that He's good and He's wise.

Today, we can trust Him as our closest Friend.
He's with us when we're feeling blue.
He's our present help and our future hope.
He is faithful, loving, and true.

Processing this Book With Your Child

What did this book make you feel? (Use the emotions chart on the next page to help your child identify the emotion they are feeling.)

Why do you think Emma's mommy was so sad? Why do you think Emma was sad? (Young children often project their thoughts onto fictional char-acters, so asking questions about the character may give your child an opportunity to share how he or she is feeling. For example, your child may express that Emma feels angry because her mommy won't play with her, even though that is not Emma's primary emotion in the book. Use this as an opportunity to discuss how your child is processing the loss of their sibling.)

What questions do you have about the loss of your baby brother or sister?

When do you miss the baby the most?

What do you think the baby would have been like?

Emma and her mommy got a Christmas stocking for the baby and talked about him when they were sad. How do you think we can remember the baby together?

What am I Feeling?

Happy

Sad

Excited

Confused

Brave

Tired

Surprised

Worried

Lonely

Jealous

Angry

Proud

What is the Gospel?

THE WORD "GOSPEL" MEANS "GOOD NEWS."

The gospel is the most beautiful story in the whole world! God created the world and everything in it and made it good. He also made people, and He loved them very much.

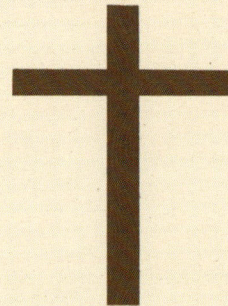

BUT THE PEOPLE DISOBEYED GOD.

THIS IS CALLED SIN.

We all disobey God, and the punishment for our sin is death. Thankfully, God had a plan from the beginning to save His people. We deserve to die for our sins, but the gospel says that God sent His Son, Jesus, to take our place. Jesus, who never sinned, died on the cross for us. Three days later, He came alive again! If we believe this good news and trust Jesus to save us, God forgives us, and we can live forever with Him.

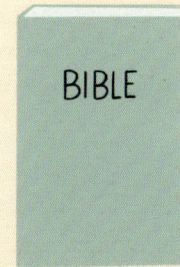

BIBLE

**WHEN WE TRUST IN JESUS,
GOD CHANGES OUR HEARTS.**

He forgives us, makes us clean, and sends His Spirit to live inside us. He makes us His sons and daughters. He protects, loves, and cares for us. In response, we want to live in a way that makes Him happy. Doing good things doesn't save us. We don't obey God to make Him love us. He loves us always and forever! Instead, we obey God because we love Him.

WE CAN LEARN MORE ABOUT GOD AND WHAT HE LOVES THROUGH THE MOST IMPORTANT BOOK OF ALL, THE BIBLE.

The Bible tells us that one day, Jesus is coming again to make everything right. He will wipe away all our tears, and there will be no more pain or sadness. He will make everything good again.

If you trust in Jesus, don't keep this good news to yourself.
Tell someone about Jesus today!